UNDAUNTED

STUDY GUIDE

CHRISTINE CAINE
with Sherry Harney

UNDAUNTED

Daring to do what God calls you to do

ZONDERVAN®

ZONDERVAN.com/
AUTHORTRACKER
follow your favorite authors

ZONDERVAN

Undaunted Study Guide
Copyright © 2012 by Christine Caine

This title is also available as a Zondervan ebook. Visit www.zondervan.com/ebooks.

Requests for information should be addressed to:

Zondervan, *Grand Rapids, Michigan 49530*

ISBN 978-0-310-89292-2

Published in association with the literary agency of David O. Middlebrook, 4501 Merlot Avenue, Grapevine, Texas 76051.

Cover design: *Grey Matter Group*
Cover photography: *Veer*® / *Corbis*® / © *Daniel H. Bailey*
Interior design: *Sarah Johnson and David Conn*

Printed in the United States of America

14 15 16 17 18 19 /DCI/ 20 19 18 17 16 15 14 13 12 11 10 9 8 7

Contents

The Moment

My wake-up moment came on a Wednesday afternoon in March 2010. Until that day I had been unaware of the evil lurking closer than I possibly could have known. I was blind. I was ignorant. But when the light was turned on and I saw things as they really were, I would never be the same.

I sat in a safe house in Greece, face-to-face with fourteen young women who had recently been rescued from unimaginable lives as sex slaves. Each of them, from various parts of the world, had been lied to, enticed, deceived, and tricked into leaving their homes and families for a "better life." Each had been brutally beaten, repeatedly raped, crushed in spirit, and then forced to work in a brothel, performing unthinkable acts every day.

These were broken women with shattered dreams and hearts. Though rescued from the sex-trafficking industry, they were still imprisoned behind bars of fear and pain.

One of the women, Sonja, looked straight at me and asked, "Why are you here?"

I did my best to tell her about the One who had rescued me from my pain, torment, and broken past. I communicated the amazing story of God's love and explained that Jesus was the One who could bring forgiveness, peace, joy, kindness, and grace to the darkest of places and most broken of hearts. I explained that he wants to set us free from physical, emotional, and spiritual dungeons. I tried to help her and the other women understand that God is so good he not only offers us a new beginning, but wants to use us to be his agents of hope, forgiveness, and grace to others who need to be rescued.

"That's why I'm here. That is why I have come," I explained.

Sonja's eyes filled with tears as she looked intently at me and asked a question that still haunts me to this day.

"Then why didn't you come sooner?"

I did my best to answer a question that can't be adequately answered. More importantly, I explained to Sonja and the thirteen others that I would do everything I could to help women like them. I promised that I would tell their story to anyone who would listen.

That moment shaped the future of my life as I knew it. I was already passionate about building God's church and seeing people come to Christ, but I became even more aware of a different aspect of God's heart for justice ... and his passion to use his church in order to see the outworking of it. This is why my husband and I started The A21 Campaign, and it played a large role in why I wrote the book, *Undaunted*. God has placed a call on my life and I will be relentless to follow that call as long as I have breath.

In the five sessions of this study, you will be invited and challenged to listen for and hear the voice of God in your life. None of us can do *everything*, but all of us can do *something*. My "something" is to build God's church as well as to help mobilize his bride to be part of the fight to eradicate human trafficking. Your call might be different. But each one of us can do our part to overcome the pain and injustices of this world. My prayer is that you will hear the voice of God speaking to you and that you will respond with an undaunted commitment and spirit.

Together, as we each do our part, the world can change as the love and grace of God flow through us to the broken and hurting next door and at the ends of the earth.

Christine Caine

OF NOTE

The quotes interspersed through this study guide are either excerpts from the book *Undaunted* by Christine Caine or from the DVD curriculum of the same name. All other resources—including the small group questions, activities, introductions, and between-sessions materials—have been written by Sherry Harney in collaboration with Christine Caine.

The Call

INTRODUCTION

Have you ever walked into a place and been shocked as people popped out from behind the doors and furniture and shouted, "Surprise!" at the top of their lungs? If you have, you know the feeling of being both startled and delighted at the same time. Once your heart rate drops to normal, the adrenaline stops coursing through your veins, and you realize what is happening, you are delighted that these people have gathered to celebrate your birthday or other special event. They have planned, communicated, and gathered to surprise you and let you know you are loved.

Everyone enjoys a surprise ... when the news is good.

Sometimes we face a moment when we receive news that startles us and redefines our life. With one line, a letter in the mail, a text message, or conversation, the landscape of our future looks completely different.

A woman receives a call from her doctor's office asking her to come in so they can review the results of the mammogram she had a few weeks earlier. She senses the news is not good, but has to wait two days to meet with the doctor. When she gets the report and learns that she has cancer, she enters a time of asking, *Who am I, and what does my future hold?*

An employee who has devoted fifteen years to the same company opens an envelope from his boss which begins, "We want to thank you for your years of service," and ends with, "we are downsizing, and your position has been removed." The words on this single sheet of paper cause him to wonder, *Am I the same person now that my job is gone?*

How should we respond when we face a moment that makes us feel we are not who we thought we were? Where do we look when the foundation of our life seems to shake, crack, and crumble beneath our feet?

TALK ABOUT IT (5 MINUTES)

Tell about a time when you were surprised with good news or by something that brought joy to your life. How did this surprise impact your life?

Or

Tell about a time when you were surprised with hard news or faced a painful situation that seemed to redefine your future.

VIDEO TEACHING NOTES (15 MINUTES)

As you watch the DVD teaching segment for session 1, use the following outline to record anything that stands out to you.

The day Christine's life turned upside down

Building your life on the truth of God's Word: John 8:31–32

Fearfully and wonderfully made in the image of God:
Psalm 139:13–14

God has a plan and a purpose and a destiny for us

We are who God says we are

Stability in changing circumstances: Romans 8:37–39

Bringing love to a lost and broken world

Life will eventually turn every person upside down, inside out. No one is immune. Not you. Not me. But just as life will up-end you, so will love.

GROUP STUDY AND DISCUSSION (30 MINUTES)

1. Christine talks about how she experienced God's presence and peace in the midst of receiving shocking and painful news. How have you felt the presence of God and his sustaining power right in the middle of a hard time in your life?

2. **Read:** Psalm 139:1–6, 13–16. What do you learn about God in this passage? What do you learn about yourself?

How can an unshakable confidence in the truth of this passage help us in times when we receive shocking and life-altering news?

3. What are some of the things that people in our world tend to use to establish their sense of value, identity, and purpose in life? Why is it dangerous to base our worth on these sorts of things?

Christine talks about how in a single moment, when she learned she was adopted, everything in her life changed. Yet, in a very real sense, nothing changed. Her fundamental identity was still the same. What are the things about you that will never change, no matter what you face, because of who you are in Christ?

When you believe God is who he says he is, when you hang onto him and his Word in faith, his truth sets you free. The truth you store up in silence comes back to you in the storm, and it lifts you away as on a life raft from the fears and disappointments that would otherwise pull you down.

4. **Read:** John 8:31–32. Jesus told his followers that the truth would set them free. What are some of the things that God declares are true about you and me? How can holding to these truths in the tough and uncertain times of life help us maintain a clear sense of who we are?

5. The Bible tells us that God's works are marvelous. God made you and me. This means we are marvelous! Tell something marvelous about yourself. Why is it so hard, in a day-to-day way, to see ourselves as marvelous in God's sight and truly valuable?

If your group is familiar with one another, share something marvelous you see in the person sitting to your right.

6. **Read:** Genesis 1:24–31. The pinnacle of God's creation is people. In Genesis God makes the stars, seas, plants, and animals and calls them "good." On the sixth day, when God created people, he said they were "very good"! God has a plan, purpose, and destiny for your life. How can you learn to identify and begin following God's plan for your life? What gets in the way of your doing so?

If you have gained some direction and clarity concerning God's plan and destiny for your life, share what you have received with your group members. Let them know how they can encourage you and pray for you as you seek to follow God's plan.

The pinnacle of God's creation is people, every single person on earth. We are God's sons and daughters created in his image with a plan and a purpose for our lives.

7. When Christine says, "We are not a product of time, we are a product of eternity," what is she getting at? What does it mean to know you are a product of eternity?

   How can this outlook change the way we view ourselves? How can it shape the way we love and treat others?

God has plucked us out of eternity, he has positioned us in time, and he has given us gifts and talents for the purpose of serving our generation.

8. **Read:** Romans 8:37–39. What are some of the things the enemy tries to use to separate us from God's love? What truth can we speak to combat these lies?

17

9. The love of God will carry and sustain you, even in the hard times. How have you experienced that reality? Tell about a time when you experienced the sustaining love of God.

What is an area of life in which you need your group members to support you in realizing the sustaining love of God? How can they pray for you?

10. What are the things that can get in the way of our bringing the love and grace of God to a broken world? What tends to get in *your* way?

What is one step you can take to share God's love in a tangible way with someone God has placed in your life?

God's love will carry you. God's love will sustain you. And, in fact, that love will cause you to soar and fulfill your God-given destiny and purpose. And when you know that love, when you know it deeply, then you can't help but love others.

PERSONAL REFLECTION (5 MINUTES)

Complete this activity on your own.

In the space provided, write down four words that describe how you think about yourself in the flow of a normal day, followed by a short sentence that tells why you feel that way. Be honest. The words you list can be positive or negative.

EXAMPLE:
Word One: Driven.
I love to accomplish tasks, but sometimes my relationships suffer because of it.

Word One:

Word Two:

Word Three:

Word Four:

Do you see yourself as fearfully and wonderfully made, of tremendous worth to God? What keeps you from seeing yourself this way? What helps you to see yourself as valuable and precious in God's sight?

GROUP PRAYER (5 MINUTES)

Spend time in your group praying in any of the following directions:

- Thank God for being with you in the surprising and painful times you have faced in your life.
- Praise God for loving you even when you feel unlovely and in the times when others have treated you as if you are not valuable.
- Pray that you will see yourself as God sees you and ask for an unshakable confidence that you are loved by God and precious in his sight.
- Ask God to help you see others the way God sees them. Pray that you will value others as "very good," and that you can help them see how beautiful they are to God.
- Thank God for the members in your group and pray that they will know how marvelous they are in God's eyes.
- Ask the Holy Spirit to open your eyes to God's plan for your life and pray for the power to follow this plan no matter what the devil tries to throw in your way. Pray that you will be undaunted in your passion to pursue God's purpose for your life.

Even if our circumstances on earth change, it doesn't mean that God's eternal plan for our lives has changed.

■ BETWEEN SESSIONS ■

Read: The introduction and chapter 1 of the *Undaunted* book. Use the space below to briefly record any thoughts; then bring your insights and questions to the next group meeting.

1. PERSONAL HISTORY ... MOMENTS OF CRISIS AND CLARITY

In her early thirties, Christine hit a crisis moment when she discovered that she and her brother were adopted. This led to a time of clarity about who she was and who God would be in her life. Using the chart on pages 22–23, think through your own life and identify some of the clarifying moments you have faced. God can use these moments to strengthen you and draw you closer to him.

SEASON OF LIFE	THE MOMENT OF CRISIS	HOW I RESPONDED
Christine's example	Discovering she was adopted	Shock; offered baklava; declaration of trust in God
In my childhood		
In my teenage years		
In my young adult years		
Later in life		

HOW GOD WAS WITH ME	HOW GOD FORMED ME
A clear feeling that she was still wonderfully made and that all her days were in God's hands	Her awareness that her value and identity are based in Christ was forged. Her compassion for the oppressed and forgotten was deepened.

2. IDENTITY CLARIFICATION

Study Psalm 139 and reflect on the identity of David (the psalmist), God, and you.

Clarifying the Identity of God: As you read this psalm, list what you learn about the heart and identity of God.

-
-
-
-
-

Clarifying the Identity of David: As you read this psalm, list what you learn about how David saw God, the world, and ultimately himself.

-
-
-
-

Clarifying Your Identity: As you read this psalm, list what you learn about yourself in relationship to God.

-
-
-
-

Reflections on Your Identity: How does this biblical view of who you are compare to how you see yourself? What thought patterns might you need to change so that your view of yourself comes into harmony with how God sees you and what the Bible teaches about you?

3. IDENTIFYING WHY GOD HAS ME ON THIS EARTH

In this session Christine says some things that might feel surprising to many people, such as:

God has a plan for your life.
God has a purpose for each of us.
God has a destiny for you.
God's love will cause you to soar and to fulfill all he has planned for you.

Think about this idea that God has a unique, wonderful, and powerful plan for your life. Dare to believe that God desires to do something in and through you for his glory, for the blessing of others, and for your good. He has a plan for you to make a difference in your home, your community, your church, and even the world. Use some of the sentence starters below to direct your thoughts:

Some of the unique and God-given abilities I have are ...

cont.

When I get some free time, I love doing the following things ...

People have told me I am good at ...

When I do the following things, I really feel the presence of God in me and the power of God working through me ...

I would want to be remembered for ...

I find deep and abiding joy when I ...

My spiritual gifts (see Romans 12; 1 Corinthians 13) are ...

Use these answers to start a composite sketch of what your passion, purpose, and calling from God might be. You don't have to nail this down right now, but begin forming a picture in your heart and mind. Over the five sessions of the *Undaunted* study, pray that God will clarify this picture.

When you are grounded and rooted in the deep love of Jesus, no matter what happens to you, no matter what news you find out about your life, you can rest in that love.

4. JOURNAL

Either in the space provided or in a separate notebook, write your reflections on any of the following topics:

- How I see myself
- How God sees me (look at Genesis 1 and Psalm 139)
- How God wants to shape and change the way I see myself
- Some ways in which I need to learn to love people the way God does
- Steps I can take to share God's love with people who don't understand how valuable they are to God

_____

_____

_____

_____

_____

_____

session 2

Be the Love

CHECKING IN FROM SESSION 1

Before beginning session 2, briefly check in with each other about your experiences since the last session.

- What questions or insights did you discover in the personal study or in the chapters you read from the *Undaunted* book?
- How did the last session impact your life?

INTRODUCTION

Names are important. Many parents think, talk, and even pray about what to name a child before she or he is born.

Often parents pick a name that has meaning to the family. A beloved grandmother is honored when a granddaughter bears her name. A father who lost a younger brother to a tragic accident in their teenage years passes the name on to a first-born son. A newborn boy carries the same name as his father and becomes "Junior" or even "The Third."

In biblical times names were very significant. Sometimes God even gave people a new name. Abram had his name divinely changed to Abraham. Sarai also received her new name Sarah by divine command. When Jesus met Simon the son of Jonah, he changed his name to Peter (meaning "rock"). Jesus himself had a name that bore significance beyond what most people in his day understood. The name Jesus means "Savior."

In our day, it is easy to find a pile of books and a list of websites that will tell you the meaning of specific names. For instance, if you do a quick search on the name Christine, you will find that it means "follower of Christ." Have you ever researched the meaning of your own name?

TALK ABOUT IT (5 MINUTES)

Tell about any family history or special meaning associated with your name or the name of another family member (first, middle, or last). How does this history add significance to your name?

Or

Tell about one way you are like your dad or mom (it could be in temperament, a physical trait, etc.). Why is some kind of connection with our parents important?

VIDEO TEACHING NOTES (15 MINUTES)

As you watch the DVD teaching segment for session 2, use the following outline to record anything that stands out to you.

I am not who I thought I was

Unnamed and just a number

The power of the truth of God's Word: Isaiah 49:1

Abuse defined

We are God's workmanship

We must value every person we meet

There is a plan, a purpose, and a destiny for each of us

God uses ordinary people to do extraordinary things: Abraham, Sarah, Noah, Miriam, Jacob, Jonah, David, Elijah, Peter, Martha, Thomas, Lazarus

God chooses you and me

Often the very things that you think have disqualified you are the ones that qualify you to do what God has called you to do.

GROUP STUDY AND DISCUSSION (30 MINUTES)

1. Christine tells about looking at her adoption papers and reading "unnamed" where her name should have been. She saw that she was just a number when the adoption papers were processed. Tell about a time when it seemed as if you were just a number or an unknown face in a crowd. How did this make you feel?

2. Christine recalls how the tape recorder went off in her mind when she learned this news. It was like the Enemy began to speak lies and destructive words to her heart telling her she was worthless. What are some of the lies the enemy tries to slip into our minds to discourage us and tear us down? What can we do to fight against these deceptive lies?

3. Read the passages below. What does God say about the worth of a person who has come to him through faith in Jesus? Briefly discuss what these truths mean to you.

John 15:13–15

Galatians 3:26–29

1 Peter 2:4–5

1 Peter 2:9–10

When there is a fight between your heart and your head, experience has taught me that the best thing you can do is pick up your Bible and remind yourself of what God says.

4. Who is a person God uses to speak words of truth and blessing to you? Why is this person so valuable in your life?

Who is one person you could speak words of blessings to in the coming week?

5. Describe a time when you felt God's presence amidst a very painful or challenging experience. How did God specifically show his love to you?

6. Christine says we must build our lives on the truth of God's Word, not on what others say about us. How is the message of the Bible different from the messages we typically receive from most people? What can we do to make sure we are getting our sense of identity from God and not the world?

If you want to find peace, you need to return to the truth of God's Word that will last forever, not meditate on the facts of your circumstances that will change and fade.

7. **Read:** Ephesians 2:4–10. What does this passage teach us about God and about ourselves? What does it mean to declare and believe that we are God's workmanship?

What are some of the "good works" God has called you to do with your life?

8. **Read:** Romans 8:1–2, 31–39. What does this passage teach you about who God is and who you are in relationship to him? If you are confident these words about you are true, how might this impact the way you see and treat other people?

9. Christine says, "God likes to show off through ordinary people." Who are some of the ordinary or even messed-up people God used in the Bible, and how are their lives testimonies of how God can use people like you and me?

10. In 1 Samuel 13:14 we read that David was "a man after [God's] own heart." We also know that he stumbled deep in sin (2 Samuel 11). How could David struggle with sin

and still be a man after God's own heart? How does David's story bring hope and encouragement to you?

> *The good news is it's not too late to turn back and to follow the path that God has chosen for your life.*

11. When we discover God's plan, purpose, and destiny for our lives, our whole outlook changes. What can we do to grow in our understanding and awareness of God's plan for each of our lives?

When we recognize and embrace God's plan, purpose, and destiny for our lives, we begin to look at other people with new eyes of love and grace. How has your outlook on people grown more loving and compassionate as your faith in Jesus deepens? What is one area in which you feel God still wants you to grow, and how can your group members pray for you and encourage you as you mature in this area?

PERSONAL REFLECTION (5 MINUTES)

Complete this activity on your own.

Who are people I can walk right past and not really acknowledge or treat with the love and value God assigns to them?

What can I do in the coming week not only to notice these people but to extend to them the love and grace of Jesus?

You and I are chosen for a purpose, we are healed for a purpose, we are called for a purpose, and that purpose always involves other people.

GROUP PRAYER (5 MINUTES)

Spend time in your group praying in any of the following directions:

- Thank God that he has made you unique and valuable. Praise him that he also values all the people around you.
- Ask the Holy Spirit to help you see the purpose, plan, and destiny God has in store for you.
- Pray for courage to love, as Jesus loved, those who are often marginalized, and ask for strength to extend his grace to those who are often forgotten.
- Thank God that he knows your name and that he sees you as his precious child and never as a number.
- Ask for a daily awareness of your value as a loved child of God so that you can look at every person you meet as important and valuable in God's eyes and your own.

■ BETWEEN SESSIONS ▬▬▬▬▬▬

Read: Chapters 2 and 3 of the *Undaunted* book. Use the space below to briefly record any thoughts; then bring your insights and questions to the next group meeting.

1. MY PURPOSE, PLAN, AND DESTINY

As you spend "alone time" with God, ask him to continue his work of clarifying his plan for your life. Finish any of the following statements, inviting God to use this process to help you embrace what he would have you do:

I have seen God use me for his glory when I . . .

Others have told me that God uses me in their lives when I . . .

These are some of the unique abilities and gifts God has given to me . . .

I take great delight and find joy when I ...

What do my reflections teach me about God's purpose, plan, and destiny for my life?

2. BECOMING FRIENDS WITH IMPERFECT PEOPLE

Study the lives of two of the following Bible characters. Pick two that seem interesting to you. Use the space provided to write your reflections:

Abraham (Genesis 12)

Sarah (Genesis 16)

Noah (Genesis 9)

Miriam (Exodus 2:1–10; 15:1–21; Numbers 12)

Jacob (Genesis 27)

Jonah (Jonah 1–4)

David (1 Samuel 16–20; 2 Samuel 7, 11–12)

Elijah (1 Kings 19)

Peter (John 18:15–27; 21:1–23)

Paul/Saul (Acts 9:1–32)

Martha (Luke 10:38–42)

Thomas (John 20:24–31)

Study #1
Name of character: _____
What were some of this person's frailties and weaknesses?

cont.

Why might he or she have felt disqualified to be used by God?

How did God work in and through the life of this person, even though he or she had weaknesses, made mistakes, and sinned against God?

What do you learn from the way God used this person?

Study #2
Name of character: _____
What were some of this person's frailties and weaknesses?

Why might he or she have felt disqualified to be used by God?

How did God work in and through the life of this person, even though he or she had weaknesses, made mistakes, and sinned against God?

What do you learn from the way God used this person?

3. EXTENDING HONOR

Take time in the coming week to think about some of the ways you have been shaped and formed. Who are the people God has used in your life to make you who you are today (family members, friends, teachers, pastors, others)? Where have you picked up some of your better mannerisms, disposition, and outlook on life?

Write notes or emails to a few of these people if they are still living. Let them know how God has used them and that you are thankful for their contribution to your life.

4. JOURNAL

Either in the space provided or in a separate notebook, write your reflections on any of the following topics:

- How God views imperfect and broken people, and how that should affect the way I believe God sees me
- In what ways I treat people as numbers and why

- How I can truly notice the people around me, see their value, and extend love and grace to them each day
- Understanding who I am "in Christ"

_____

_____

_____

_____

_____

_____

_____

_____

_____

_____

_____

_____

_____

_____

_____

_____

_____

_____

_____

_____

_____

Be the Hope

CHECKING IN FROM SESSION 2

Before beginning session 3, briefly check in with each other about your experiences since the last session.

- What questions or insights did you discover in the personal study or in the chapters you read from the *Undaunted* book?
- How did the last session impact your life?

INTRODUCTION

The twentieth-century American educator and author Loren Eiseley wrote a short piece titled "The Starfish Story" or "The Star Thrower," which has been told and retold in many versions through the years. In this classic tale, we learn a simple lesson about the difference one person can make. Here's the gist of the story:

A man walking along an otherwise deserted beach came upon another man throwing into the sea a starfish that had been deposited on the sand by the tide. When the man asked the star thrower his purpose, the thrower explained that the starfish, left untended, would be dried by the sun and eventually die. But how, wondered the first man, could the starfish thrower ever hope to make a difference given that there were thousands of starfish scattered for miles along the beach. The thrower bent down, picked up another starfish, and threw it into the ocean with all his might. He smiled as he said, "It makes a difference for this one."

People tell this story because it invites us to believe that we can make a difference in the world. Even when the challenges we face seem daunting and bigger than we can navigate, we want to dare to do something and believe that God can use one person to change the world.

In stark contrast is the cartoon that depicts forty or fifty round faces looking straight ahead. Over each face is a text bubble with the same five words: "What can one person do?" It's just such an attitude that can poison our souls and keep us from making a difference in the world.

TALK ABOUT IT (5 MINUTES)

Tell about a person you have met who is a starfish thrower, always trying to do his or her part to make a difference in the world.

Or

What can cause people to think and say, "What can one person do"?

VIDEO TEACHING NOTES (15 MINUTES)

As you watch the DVD teaching segment for session 3, use the following outline to record anything that stands out to you.

Confronted with evil: unprepared for Auschwitz

Silence in the midst of suffering

The Holy Spirit awakens me

When God's people sleep through injustice, the darkness just gets darker

"The Spirit of the Lord is on me" (Luke 4:18)

The danger of getting consumed with our own life

It's time to wake up: Ephesians 5:14

It's time to shine: Matthew 5:14–16

> *God's glory is upon us. It can break through the darkest night. It is in us ready to burst out and overwhelm the darkness. That is what light does. It makes the darkness disappear.*

GROUP STUDY AND DISCUSSION (30 MINUTES)

1. When Christine walked through Auschwitz and was faced with the reality of what happened to thousands of Jewish people in that concentration camp and many others like it, she was changed for life. Describe a time when you were confronted by the depth of human sin and evil and how this experience has shaped the way you see the world today. How can looking honestly at the pain and suffering of this world move us to action?

2. Christine reflects on the reality that many people have fallen asleep to suffering, injustice, and evil in our world. What causes us to become passive toward these things?

What can wake us up to a new way of seeing the world and a new way of living that will move us into world-changing actions?

3. Christine warns, "We can be consumed with the personal, with the immediate, and with having our needs met." How have you experienced this in your life? What can we do to make sure this does not happen to us?

4. **Read:** Luke 4:14–21. This passage, quoted from Isaiah 61, is a prophecy fulfilled in Jesus Christ, the One who brought freedom to all who will believe in him and receive his amazing grace. Now reread verses 18–19 several times on your own, slowly and reflectively.

> "The Spirit of the Lord is on *me*, because he has anointed *me* to proclaim good news to the poor. He has sent *me* to proclaim freedom for the prisoners and recovery of sight for the blind, to set the oppressed free, to proclaim the year of the Lord's favor."

Each time this passage uses the word *me*, it is referring to who Jesus was and what he did. But if we, as his followers, are to think and live like Jesus, it also refers to us. Tell your group members one way your life might change if you woke up each morning quoting this short passage and believing that it should direct your day.

5. How does investing our time, talents, and treasures in God's priorities help others in need and lead to a deeper and richer faith in Jesus? Sometimes we ignore the needs of others and sleepwalk past the injustices in our world. How can this attitude and lifestyle weaken our faith?

> *It's time to understand that there is a greater power, the power of the resurrected Christ living on the inside of us, that enables us to bring transformation to the world around us.*

6. **Read:** Romans 13:11–14. What spiritual realities are affirmed in this passage? What does this passage call us to do? What does it warn us to avoid and run away from?

7. God cautions us to be careful not to waste the limited time we have in this life. What are some time-wasters that can soak up many hours of our days? What can we do to ensure that we are investing our time and energy on things that matter and make an eternal difference?

8. **Read:** Ephesians 5:8–20. In this passage God calls his people to "Wake up!" What are some things we can do to ensure that we stay awake and attuned to the things God wants us to do? How can we help wake each other up?

9. **Read:** Matthew 5:14–16. How has God uniquely equipped his people to bring light into dark places? How can you and your group members get engaged in shining light in the places of darkness in your community, your nation, and the world?

Unless we proactively make a decision to take the light of Christ, the hope of Christ, the good news of Jesus into a lost and broken world, then injustice will continue to prevail.

10. Christine's daughter innocently said, "Can we please go and find some darkness?" The church should be in the business of doing exactly this. How can your church (and other churches) do its job of finding, entering, and battling the darkness?

Light works best in one place, and that's in the midst of darkness.

PERSONAL REFLECTION (5 MINUTES)

Complete this activity on your own.

What is my natural disposition when it comes to how I see the challenges in the world and how I respond to them? Am I busy throwing starfish back into the ocean, or do I tend to spend my time saying, "What can one person do?"

When was a time I really got in the game, shined my light into the darkness, and tried to make a difference for Jesus in a place of real pain and suffering? How did this make me feel? How did this impact my attitude and life?

What is one place of injustice, pain, suffering, and darkness in my community or the world that I tend to avoid or ignore? Why do I shy away from this? How can I begin praying for God to lead me and other committed Christians into this place of darkness?

> *Switch on the light. Your world around you is waiting for you to shine the light of Christ and dispel the darkness.*

GROUP PRAYER DIRECTION (5 MINUTES)

Spend time in your group praying in any of the following directions:

- Pray that you will be a person who throws starfish and not someone who says, "What can one person do?"
- Pray that your church will be a force for good and God's hope right in the community where God has placed you.
- Ask God to send workers into the harvest fields, beginning with you.
- Ask God to wake up Christians around you who might be sleepwalking and not even know it. Pray that God will wake you up, if this prayer applies to you.
- Invite the Holy Spirit to be so alive in your heart and home that you will shine like a light on a hill.

Once the prison door has been opened I, who have been freed, have a responsibility to go and free others.

■ BETWEEN SESSIONS ■

Read: Chapters 4, 5, and 6 of the *Undaunted* book. Use the space below to briefly record any thoughts; then bring your insights and questions to the next group meeting.

1. MEET A NEIGHBOR

Christine talks about how we can become isolated and not even engage with those who live near us. This keeps us from seeing their struggles and the darkness in which they live. In turn, we are not able to bring God's light to them.

During the coming week, meet a neighbor whom you have never met. Or, spend time with a neighbor with whom you have not connected on a deep level for some time. You might want to bake some cookies or give a small thoughtful gift. Find time to connect, listen with a prayerful heart, and look for an opportunity to shine God's light right where you live.

2. SMELLING SALTS

Have you ever seen (in real life, on TV, or in a movie) when a boxer is knocked out? Sometimes someone will get smelling salts and place them under the nose of the unconscious fighter. All of a sudden he jolts into consciousness.

God wants us to wake up and see the needs of the world around us. He also wants us to help others wake up. We can be his smelling salts for other Christians. In a way, session 3 of the *Undaunted* curriculum is God's way of using Christine as his smelling salts to awaken you and your fellow group members.

Pray about how God might use you to awaken another Christian to some of the needs in the world or your community. This could be done in many ways:

- Have coffee with another believer, telling that person what you learned in this study and how it was a wake-up call for you.
- Give another Christian a copy of the *Undaunted* book, inviting him or her to read it and then meet with you later to discuss questions and insights.
- Invite a friend or another couple to your small group the next time you meet (if it is an open group) so they might hear the things you are learning.
- If you or your group engages in some kind of outreach project where you seek to bring the grace and light of Jesus, invite someone who is not in your group to come along with you.

3. THROW A STARFISH ONCE A DAY FOR A WEEK

Using the following chart, create a list of little things you can do for others, one each day for a week. These can be small acts of service, engaging in prayer for those who are oppressed, visiting a person who has been forgotten, or some other action you discussed with your group. Keep this small and doable. Then follow through!

Day 1	Action:	Completed:
Day 2	Action:	Completed:
Day 3	Action:	Completed:
Day 4	Action:	Completed:
Day 5	Action:	Completed:
Day 6	Action:	Completed:
Day 7	Action:	Completed:

4. JOURNAL

Either in the space provided or in a separate notebook, write your reflections on any of the following topics:

- The dark places I see in my community or world
- Ways I have tried to bring the hope and light of Jesus into dark places
- Ways I can live out the example of Jesus found in Luke 4:18–21
- How God is waking me up to the needs, hurts, and injustices in the world
- How God is using me, my group, and his church to bring hope and light to the world

_____

_____

_____

_____

_____

_____

_____

_____

_____

_____

_____

_____

_____

_____

session 4

Be the Change

CHECKING IN FROM SESSION 3

Before beginning session 4, briefly check in with each other about your experiences since the last session.

- What questions or insights did you discover in the personal study or in the chapters you read from the *Undaunted* book?
- How did the last session impact your life?

INTRODUCTION

You might have seen a milk carton with a picture of a missing child on the back. Included is a brief description of the little boy or girl and information about where he or she was last seen. Similar posters are often placed in a post office or other government offices, sometimes even at a supermarket or shopping mall.

Have you ever stopped to really read the information about that child on the milk carton? Have you looked into her eyes and wondered where she is today, how her parents are feeling, if she will ever come home again? Or, is it easier to turn the carton around so you don't have to stare into those eyes while you're eating your cornflakes?

What might change if the picture of that boy or girl was someone you knew personally? How would you respond if the face on that milk carton or post office wall was your own child, grandchild, or the daughter or son of a close and dear friend? Could you still walk past the poster or eat your cereal without being moved in some way?

TALK ABOUT IT (5 MINUTES)

What do you find is your typical response to pictures or news reports of missing people?

Or

Imagine that someone you love and know well was abducted. How would you feel? What would you do? In what ways would you pray?

VIDEO TEACHING NOTES (15 MINUTES)

As you watch the DVD teaching segment for session 4, use the following outline to record anything that stands out to you.

Missing

Twenty-seven million slaves on earth

Looking into the eyes of a real person

The Good Samaritan: Luke 10:25 – 37

Too busy to be inconvenienced and interrupted

Compassion defined

Excuses and "limitations"

Cross the street: Responding to divine interruptions

You can't do everything, but you can do something.

GROUP STUDY AND DISCUSSION (30 MINUTES)

1. Tell about a time when you were surprised or shocked by the reality of some particular injustice or oppression in our world, or when you became aware of a group of people who are regularly forgotten, ignored, or marginalized.

So many have no way out, unless we go to rescue them.

2. Statistics as large as those Christine has mentioned can desensitize and overwhelm us. But we are moved in a new way when we know the name of one real person who is facing a future of slavery. Christine talks about "the power of one." What is she getting at? How can we think about one person's needs in a way that moves us to actions that bring freedom, healing, and justice?

3. **Read:** Luke 10:25–37. What do you learn about the priest and the Levite in this passage? How are we tempted to act similarly when we face unexpected needs? What are some of the ways we pass by on the other side of the road?

What strikes you about the Good Samaritan in this passage? What were the specific ways he responded to the unexpected need he faced that day as he traveled down the road?

Very often we see hurting people as an interruption to our day instead of the object of God's will for our life.

4. We can't meet *every* need we encounter. But we can do our part, each day, as the Holy Spirit leads. How can we know when God is calling us to stop and meet the needs we encounter as we travel down the road of life? What helps you discern when God is nudging you to take action?

5. Being busy and running at too fast a pace can cause us to hurry past needs right in front of us. Evaluate your pace of life. In what ways can you slow down enough to create space in your heart and schedule to cross the road and help people in need?

6. Compassion is not fundamentally about crying or feeling sad. It is not really about an emotional response. True compassion is about getting involved in others' pain and suffering and bringing the healing, hope, and restoration of Jesus to their place of need. How do you respond to this definition of compassion? How might our homes, neighborhoods, and churches change if we lived with this kind of compassion?

> *Compassion is never compassion until we cross the street and get involved in someone else's pain.*

7. Too often we make excuses for not getting involved with the needs that are all around us. We say, "But God, I can't because ..." What are some of our excuses that allow us to cross the street and walk past these needs?

What is *your* most common excuse, and is it really valid?

8. Christine talks about how God provides when we have the courage to embrace divine interruptions and appointments. What are some of the ways God can provide the following:

- Financial resources
- Wisdom and the right words

- The time or energy you need
- An open door

Tell about a time you slowed down, changed your plans, and responded to a need that God placed in front of you. How did God show up, provide, and help you?

Don't structure your days so rigidly that you lock out God from working with you in the middle of your life. Loosen up your life enough to be ready for interruptions.

9. Ultimately, people need Jesus. We can meet all kinds of outer needs, but the deepest need of the heart and what will satisfy for eternity is the hope found in Jesus alone. As we slow down, show compassion, and share his love, other lives will be changed (and so will ours!). How have you seen Jesus bring healing, hope, or restoration into the lives of people you've served?

10. What is one need you see on a regular basis and have been thinking about but have not yet responded to? How can your group members pray for you, encourage you, and keep you accountable to take action in response to this need?

How often we pray for God to use us for his purpose, and then when he interrupts our lives to answer our prayer, we begin to list all the excuses why we are inadequate.

PERSONAL REFLECTION (5 MINUTES)

Complete this activity on your own.

How do I respond to interruptions? Am I irritated? Do people know that I should never be disturbed? Do I roll with God's divine appointments or feel frustrated when someone or something pushes me off my well-planned schedule?

How can I posture my life (schedule and attitude) so that I am more prepared to embrace divine interruptions? What could change in my schedule? What might need to be adjusted in my attitude? Choose at least one action step as you move forward.

Too often, we are the answer to someone's prayer, but we miss it.

GROUP PRAYER (5 MINUTES)

Spend time in your group praying in any of the following directions:

- Pray that you will no longer be able to walk past the injustices you encounter in the flow of an ordinary day.
- Ask God to help you know what you should do and when you should act when you face the needs of the hurting and broken in your world.
- Confess where you have become too busy and ask God to help you order your life in a way that leaves space for compassionate action.
- Ask God to slow you down so you don't rush past the Spirit-ordained opportunities you face each day.
- Thank God for the people who have slowed down and ministered to you in your times of need.
- Ask God to prepare you to respond well to divine interruptions.

Ask God to transform you into his image: to see what he sees, feel what he feels, love as he loves.

■ BETWEEN SESSIONS ■

Read: Chapters 7 and 8 of the *Undaunted* book. Use the space below to briefly record any thoughts; then bring your insights and questions to the next group meeting.

1. WEB SEARCH

Research human trafficking, world hunger, and reaching unreached people groups with God's Word. Use the websites below (or others you may know of) to find articles, statistics, and possible action steps to make a difference in these areas of injustice and need.

Study #1: Human Trafficking
Websites: *www.thea21campaign.org*; *www.ijm.org*;
www.polarisproject.org

What I learned ...

Actions and ideas that could make a difference ...

Study #2: World Hunger

Websites: *www.worldvision.org*; *www.compassion.net* or
www.compassion.com

What I learned . . .

Actions and ideas that could make a difference . . .

Study #3: Bringing the Bible to Unreached Peoples

Websites: *www.worldmission.cc*; *www.wycliffe.org*

What I learned . . .

Actions and ideas that could make a difference . . .

2. THE POWER OF ONE

Allow yourself to begin to feel for and connect with one person who is facing oppression, pain, and injustice. You don't have to know this person; you may have never met. But if you see this person's face and look into his or her eyes, God can begin to break your heart for this one and for others facing the same plight.

Find a picture on one of the websites you studied in the last exercise. It could be the face of a girl who has been abducted and sold into the sex trafficking industry. It could be a little boy who lives with hunger every day. It could be a person in a part of the world who has never heard the life-giving words of Scripture. Print out a picture of this person and post it where you will see it on a regular basis. Put it in your wallet or purse. Make it a screen saver on your computer. Put it in your phone. Each time you look at this picture, ask God to use the reality of this one person's need to move you to take daily steps of love and grace that will impact one person you encounter that day.

3. MY TOP FIVE EXCUSES

List the five most common excuses that you use (in your mind or that you say out loud) to justify walking past needs. Write these excuses below:

1.

2.

3.

4.

5.

In the coming month, listen to what you say and what you are thinking. If God is leading you to meet a need with compassionate action, don't let your excuses get in the way. When you hear yourself use one of the above excuses, stop and pray. Ask God to direct your heart, mind, and hands.

Remember, we can't do everything, but we can all do something. There will be times when you are not the person God has in mind to meet a specific need. But always be ready and open. When God is leading you to bring help, healing, love, and compassion, do so.

4. JOURNAL

Either in the space provided or in a separate notebook, write your reflections on any of the following topics:

- Times when I walked past the needs of hurting and broken people and why I did so
- Any time this past month when I stopped and helped in some way and what caused me to respond to God's leading
- The hurts and needs I notice as I walk through my week
- An occasion when I felt God was seeking to interrupt my schedule to meet a need and how I responded to this divine appointment

_____

_____

_____

_____

_____

_____

_____

_____

_____

_____

_____

_____

_____

_____

_____

_____

_____

_____

_____

_____

_____

_____

_____

_____

_____

_____

_____

_____

_____

_____

session 5

The Challenge

CHECKING IN FROM SESSION 4

Before beginning session 5, briefly check in with each other about your experiences since the last session.

- What questions or insights did you discover in the personal study or in the chapters you read from the *Undaunted* book?
- How did the last session impact your life?

INTRODUCTION

Every challenge we face demands a tenacious spirit that will press through the inevitable dangers, painful difficulties, and consistent disappointments. Any person who wants to be used by God to bring about small or large transformation in this world will have to decide, "Am I willing to count the cost? Is the challenge worth the price I will pay in the hours, days, months, or even the years ahead?" If we enter God's plan to restore broken people and bring the love of Jesus into this world, we will face challenges that will stretch our abilities and limitations.

In the early 1960s, during the fury of civil tension in South Africa, Nelson Mandela continued to fight against apartheid. The challenge seemed insurmountable and resistance appeared futile. Certainly there was daily danger, difficulty, and disappointment for those resisting one of the strongest forms of institutionalized evil on the planet at the time. Mandela experienced this on a very personal level when he was thrown into prison in 1962 and left there for twenty-seven years. On February 11, 1990, when he was finally released, Nelson was ready to continue the fight.

The tenacity of Mandela and countless others in Africa and around the world who took up the challenge eventually brought apartheid (as a legal institution) crumbling to the ground. In 1993, Nelson Mandela received the Nobel Peace Prize, and in 1994, in a multiracial election, Mandela became the president of South Africa.

Every challenge we seek to overcome will have its own dangers and difficulties. If it did not, it would not be a challenge. Toppling an unjust political system, fighting human trafficking, helping the hungry in your community, reaching lost people with the love of God, visiting those who are in prison (justly or unjustly), providing education for migrant children, bringing fresh water to the thirsty, helping a neighbor in a time of crisis, and thousands of other acts of service all come with their own unique challenges. If you and I are going to make a difference for Jesus in this world, the question is not, "Will we face challenges?" The real question is, "Will we be ready to face dangers, difficulties, and disappointments and learn to press on with an undaunted spirit?"

TALK ABOUT IT (5 MINUTES)

Tell of a time when you responded to God's call to meet a specific challenge. What did you learn about God and yourself as you confronted these challenges?

Or

Tell about a danger or disappointment you faced when you accepted a challenge God placed before you. Looking back, how do you view what you sacrificed?

VIDEO TEACHING NOTES (15 MINUTES)

As you watch the DVD teaching segment for session 5, use the following outline to record anything that stands out to you.

Moved to action: The A21 Campaign

Obstacles and hurdles along the way

The question was "how," not "if"

The three Ds of facing a God-sized challenge:

- Danger
- Difficulties
- Disappointments

Overcoming our fears ... in the power of Jesus

Dealing with disappointments

Why didn't you come sooner?

The hope of the gospel ... God has a plan, purpose, and destiny for your life

Seize the day

God calls us to go into the darkness to make a difference.

GROUP STUDY AND DISCUSSION (30 MINUTES)

1. Despite others' concerns, Christine pressed on to help people trapped in the grip of human trafficking because she knew it was God's call on her life. Tell of a time you were confident that God was calling you to do something, but others were not so sure. How did you press on even though people discouraged or did not fully support you?

If God said there is a way, he will make a way where there is no way.

2. **Read:** Numbers 13:17–33. What did Moses call the twelve men to do as they explored the land of Canaan? What did the majority of these men report when they returned? How was Caleb's report and attitude different?

cont.

Those who gave the bad report delivered some honest and truthful information, but they also embellished the truth, and some of what they reported was not accurate at all. What did they report that was true, what was exaggerated, and what was false? How can fear cause us to see the challenges ahead of us in exaggerated and inaccurate ways?

3. Take two or three minutes on your own to identify one challenge you are facing (in your life, workplace, a relationship, your church, or your community). As you think about this challenge, write down *honest* and *accurate* dangers, difficulties, and potential disappointments you might face if you press on:

Dangers:

Difficulties:

Disappointments:

Now, share one or two issues with your group members. If time permits, add these concerns to your prayer time at the end of the session.

4. Christine talks about how some people live in prisons with literal bars, but many are in prisons with invisible bars. All of these people need the deliverance and hope that Jesus alone can bring. What are some of the prisons with invisible bars that people live in?

What are ways that you and other followers of Jesus can set these people free and help them experience the deliverance that only Jesus can bring?

5. We will need to overcome our fears if we are going to follow the challenges God places in front of us. What is a fear you are facing in this season of your life and how are you dealing with it? How can your group members pray and support you as you face this challenge and the fear it brings?

Every dawn is a reminder that we have a new day, another chance to make a difference.

6. **Read:** 2 Timothy 1:7 and 1 John 4:18. What do these passages tell us about fear in the heart and life of a follower of Jesus? What is the connection between love and fear?

7. Briefly describe one of your "God appointments," a time you followed God even when it was challenging, and he showed up and did something powerful that surprised you and others.

8. In an encounter with a woman caught in the world of human trafficking, Christine had the opportunity to tell her about the amazing love of God and the grace of Jesus, the Savior. How can persistent love, service, and care for the hurting in this world open the door for us to communicate the gospel message? If you have a personal story to illustrate this, share it with the group.

Standing in the gap is Jesus, who has thrown down his cross as the bridge from the world of darkness into the world of light and freedom, truth and love.

9. **Read:** Romans 8:9–11; John 17:13–19; and John 20:21. What is our source of power and strength to follow God and make a difference in this world? Where do we often look for our source of strength? Why is it critical that we remember the source of our power as we face the challenges God sets before us?

10. If we are to extend healing, we need to experience it in a deep and personal way. Tell about some of the ways God has healed or is healing you—your heart, your past, whatever. How does your experience of healing help you reach out to others with the restoring power of Jesus?

How can your group members pray for you as you continue to grow in your understanding of God's grace and healing in your life?

We who have been rescued have a responsibility to rescue others.

79

PERSONAL REFLECTION (5 MINUTES)

Complete this activity on your own.

Christine finishes this final session by assuring us that the goal of this study has not been to cause us guilt or condemnation. Instead, it is to inspire all of us to face the glorious challenges God places before us and to make a difference for Jesus in our broken and dark world.

How does guilt and condemnation actually get in the way of you fulfilling God's design and plan for your life? How can you move beyond paralyzing guilt and condemnation to God-honoring action?

Think about what Jesus did on the cross for you by meditating on Romans 8:1: "Therefore, there is now no condemnation for those who are in Christ Jesus." Write a brief prayer of praise to God to embrace the reality that you are loved and forgiven.

For when we were yet unloved, he loved us.

GROUP PRAYER (5 MINUTES)

Spend time in your group praying in any of the following directions:

- Thank God for the people he has used in your life to show you an example of courage and persistence in accepting God-ordained challenges.
- Ask the Holy Spirit to give you power and boldness to follow the challenges God is inviting you to take.
- Confess where you have been paralyzed by fear or overwhelmed by personal issues to such an extent that you have not accepted God's challenges.
- Declare to God that you will not live and walk in condemnation or guilt. Thank Jesus for washing you clean and preparing you for a great mission ahead.
- Pray for those in your church or community who are in a time of great need and hurt. Offer your time, resources, love, and life to help them as God leads you.
- If you or other group members have pain from past disappointments, pray for healing in your souls so that you will be ready to serve God and the broken people around you in the future.

Don't allow the disappointments of yesterday stop you from stepping into the God appointments of tomorrow.

■ IN THE COMING DAYS ▰▰▰▰▰▰

Read: Chapter 9 and the conclusion of the *Undaunted* book. Use the space below to briefly note any insights or questions.

1. FACING THE THREE DS

Refer back to your responses to question 3 of this session's Group Study and Discussion (page 76) regarding a challenge you are currently facing in some area of your life. Write down any additional thoughts, both positive and negative, that you had about this challenge since your meeting. Note any Scriptures (either from your own devotional reading or ones that you've recently heard preached or taught) that speak God's reassuring truth about the potential dangers, difficulties, and disappointments surrounding your challenge.

Finally, offer yourself and your challenge to God. Pray for courage to press on and ask for his love to fill you and overcome any fears that might begin to slip in. Let God know that you will follow his leading no matter what you face.

2. OBSTACLES

Many things can keep us from reaching out to people in the midst of their needs. How have you seen any of the following "internal issues" keep people (including yourself) from taking the challenge to reach out?

Unforgiveness

Bitterness

Shame

Fear

Guilt

Rejection

Hurt

Offer these to God in prayer as well.

3. PICKING A NEED

Boldly consider how you might become God's instrument to help meet one specific need in your local church or community. Use the following process to help you move forward into action:

Step 1: Pray for God's leading and direction.

Step 2: Make a list of up to a dozen different needs you are aware of in your church or local community.

- •   •
- •   •
- •   •
- •   •
- •   •
- •   •

Step 3: Talk about which of these needs you (or a group of likeminded people) could meet. How could you shine the light of Jesus and bring the love of God into this place of need? Narrow down your list to three needs.

- •
- •
- •

Step 4: Pray for wisdom and God's direction as you decide what need to meet and the specific action you should take.

Step 5: Narrow down your list to one need and clarify what action you will take, and when you will do it.

Need: _____

Action: _____

_____

_____

Step 6: Act on your commitment and follow through on the ministry you committed to do, even if you face challenges along the way.

Step 7: Pray that the seeds you planted and the grace that was extended will take root and bring fruit for God's glory and the good of those you have served.

4. JOURNAL

Either in the space provided or in a separate notebook, write your reflections on any of the following topics:

- Examples, throughout history, of people who have been bold for God, followed his divine challenge, and seen amazing fruit
- A time I accepted a challenge God placed before me and the good things he did in and through me
- The things that tend to keep me from accepting God's challenges during this season of my life
- A prayer of commitment to follow God, no matter the potential dangers, difficulties, or disappointments that might come my way
- Acts of compassion, love, and ministry I could offer to people right where God has placed me (my workplace, school, neighborhood, social activities, etc.)

Small Group Leader Helps

To ensure a successful small group experience, read the following information before beginning.

GROUP PREPARATION

Whether your small group has been meeting together for years or is gathering for the first time, be sure to designate a consistent time and place to work through the five sessions. Once you establish the when and where of your times together, select a facilitator who will keep discussions on track and an eye on the clock. If you choose to rotate this responsibility, assign the five sessions to their respective facilitators upfront, so they can prepare their thoughts and questions prior to the session they are responsible for leading. Follow the same assignment procedure should your group want to serve any snacks or beverages.

A NOTE TO FACILITATORS

As facilitator, you are responsible for honoring the agreed-upon time frame of each meeting, for prompting helpful discussion among your group, and for keeping the dialogue equitable by drawing out quieter members and helping more talkative participants to remember that others' insights are also valued in your group.

You might find it helpful to preview each session's video teaching segment and then scan the "Group Study and Discussion" questions that pertain to it, highlighting various questions that you want to be sure to cover during your group's meeting. Before your group meets, ask God to guide the discussion, and then be sensitive to the direction in which he wishes to lead.

Urge participants to bring their study guide, pen, and a Bible to every gathering. Encourage them to each consider buying a personal copy (or one per couple) of the book *Undaunted* by Christine Caine to supplement this study.

SESSION FORMAT

Each session of the *Undaunted* study is planned for about an hour, but may be expanded should your group have more time available. Every session of the study guide includes the following components:

- **Checking In** (sessions 2–5) — an opportunity to briefly revisit the previous session to raise any follow-up questions or insights
- **Introduction** — a launch point to the session's topic, which may be read by a volunteer or summarized by the facilitator
- **Talk About It** — an icebreaker question that relates to the session topic and invites input from every group member
- **Video Teaching Notes** — an outline of the session's video teaching (which lasts about 15 minutes) for group members to follow along and take notes if they wish

- **Group Study and Discussion**—video-related and Bible exploration questions that reinforce the session content and elicit personal input from every group member
- **Personal Reflection**—an opportunity for individual response to the session content
- **Group Prayer**—several prayer cues to guide group members in closing prayer

Additionally, in each session you will find a **Between Sessions** section that includes suggestions for personal response, recommended reading from the *Undaunted* book, and journaling prompts. Each personal study is divided into four portions. Group members may opt to do the personal study in one sitting or spread it out over several days.

Foreword by MAX LUCADO

CHRISTINE CAINE

UNDAUNTED

Daring to do what God calls you to do

UNDAUNTED

*Daring to do what
God calls you to do*

CHRISTINE CAINE,
Hillsong Church

We all have fears. Some fears entail facing things that have happened to us in our past; others have to do with braving the battles that lay ahead of us in the future. Christine Caine was faced with the daunting challenge of overcoming both.

At age 33, how did she deal with finding out she was adopted? How did she subvert childhood abuse? What compelled her to take up the challenge of fighting human trafficking when she had two young children and zero credentials for taking on such a global injustice?

Through UNDAUNTED, Christine Caine answers every person's excuse to run from our fears, while simultaneously giving us tools to overcome them. Her raw honesty, combined with her humor and contagious passion will dare you to live a life beyond your wildest dreams, and face even the most unexpected challenges ahead - undaunted.

THE A21 CAMPAIGN

99% OF HUMAN TRAFFICKING VICTIMS ARE NOT RESCUED... YET.

When confronted with the horrific statistics surrounding human trafficking, most people are quick to agree on the fact that someone should **do something.** The A21 Campaign was born when we decided to raise our hand and be the ones who would do something. The A21 Campaign was born when we decided to raise our hand and join the ranks of "someone." In 2007, with little knowledge and a lot of passion, we set out to make a difference. Today we are strategically positioned in Europe, North America, and Australia to abolish the injustice of human trafficking and rehabilitate victims.

The goal of A21 is fourfold:

1. Prevent people from being trafficked.

2. Protect those who have been trafficked, and provide support services.

3. Prosecute traffickers, and strengthen legal responses to trafficking.

4. Partner with law enforcement, service providers, and community members to provide a comprehensive front against trafficking.

BECA21USE... everyONE matters.

www.TheA21Campaign.org

Share Your Thoughts

With the Author: Your comments will be forwarded to the author when you send them to *zauthor@zondervan.com*.

With Zondervan: Submit your review of this book by writing to *zreview@zondervan.com*.

Free Online Resources at
www.zondervan.com

Zondervan AuthorTracker: Be notified whenever your favorite authors publish new books, go on tour, or post an update about what's happening in their lives at www.zondervan.com/ authortracker.

Daily Bible Verses and Devotions: Enrich your life with daily Bible verses or devotions that help you start every morning focused on God. Visit www.zondervan.com/newsletters.

Free Email Publications: Sign up for newsletters on Christian living, academic resources, church ministry, fiction, children's resources, and more. Visit www.zondervan.com/newsletters.

Zondervan Bible Search: Find and compare Bible passages in a variety of translations at www.zondervanbiblesearch.com.

Other Benefits: Register to receive online benefits like coupons and special offers, or to participate in research.